THE SCARBOROUGH

The Scarborough

MICHAEL LISTA

SIGNAL EDITIONS IS AN IMPRINT OF VÉHICULE PRESS

Published with the generous assistance of The Canada Council for the Arts and the Canada Book Fund of the Department of Canadian Heritage.

SIGNAL EDITIONS EDITOR: CARMINE STARNINO

Cover design: David Drummond
Photo of author: Elizabeth Lista
Set in Filosofia and Minion by Simon Garamond
Printed by Marquis Book Printing Inc.

Published by Véhicule Press, Montréal, Québec, Canada
www.vehiculepress.com

Distribution in Canada by LitDistCo
www.litdistco.ca

Distributed in the U.S. by Independent Publishers Group
www.ipgbook.com

Printed in Canada on FSC-certified paper.

for

Contents

As they drew closer, one of the silent figures stepped forward. It was an old woman, white-haired and wizened, but with a straight back and an eye as clear as a bird's.

'Why have you come to the land of the dead?' she demanded.

'We come on no harmful business, old woman,' said Coyote. 'But we have journeyed far, and we are cold and tired and hungry. Is there hospitality in this land for travelers?'

The old woman nodded slowly. 'There is a place ready for you,' she said. 'But you must close your eyes and look at nothing around you. This is a sacred place, and what happens here in this village is not for the eyes of the living.'

– "Coyote in the Land of the Dead" by Gail Robertson

Easter, 1992, Toronto

Mistletoe

Aeneas prayed while the Sibyl answered:
"Going to hell is easy. Day and night
Its door jingles like a convenience store's.
But it's a hard return, repairing home
After the sulfur and the suffering.
In any case, here's what you need to do:
On a hidden tree there's a golden bough,
Its province secret, one bough in a borough,
Its leaves and sinew gold, gold too its stem,
Held sacred to the captive Queen of Hell.
No one may know the Earth's secret places
Without first retrieving the golden bough
And offering the Queen her harrowed gift.
Detach the bough and it regenerates.
Like the severed limb that resumes its place
On T-1000, the molten leaf reforms.
Once you find it, grasp it in your hand
And pull like you are opening a drawer—
Willingly, freely, it should fall away
If fate is on your side and leads your way.
If not, no strength or force can make it budge,
Nor saw, however sharp, will shear it off."

With that two birds—one white, one black—appeared.
Perched on Aeneas's shoulders, they sang.
What secrets did they know? Where would they go?
He followed their drooping scoops between trees,
Traversing provinces, then continents,
Antitheses and mirror images,
Down Christie, which at Bloor turns into Grace,
Until they landed on my front yard's oak,
The double-natured tree Grace Street's very own.

Like mistletoe, Christ's favourite party game,
That parasite under which strangers kiss,
That poison where my two doves feed and sing,
Which lives and dies an alien on its host,
So the bough haunted the oak like its ghost.
And from my window I saw Aeneas
Climb the oak where Toronto's skyline shone
Like Tenebrae candles blown out at dawn.
So he grips the bough. But the bough fights back.
Then like an ice cream truck, or knife sharpener,
All hell comes jingling from a tiny crack.

I

FRIDAY

The Scarborough Bluffs

You will not find me among the women of the earth,
Their hair wound up in buns upon their heads,
And goosebumped legs bridged above the bath—

I am not with them. But let it not be said
That an Orpheus doesn't sound them
That behind me suddenly he isn't

Eurydice, his the face to which I may not
Turn and look, *or else*
As prayers of rescue rise to no messiah.

Decades later and a block away
The Alzheimer takes off her glasses and her coat
And half-naked amid the snow she lays

In the cedar-ribbed hull of a boat
On neighbourless Lake Gibson, June, as five
Stone blocks of thought leopard the lakebed.

And all alone tonight I'll drive
These empty streets
And for the first time in forever feel alive,

Feel the secular roar of the Gardiner,
And smile at how in the land of the nightmask
Mascara is a kind of queenmaker.

I leave the zoo with the moon on the park,
The wolves asleep, the lions going down
(even the sun leaves Scarborough before it's dark)

And the lot of us descend to the Bluffs,
The keloid scar where a wound has frescoed
Over the vanishing land's gag order to the south.

A figure in the varves emerges like Francesca
From Rodin's *Gates of Hell*. We discandy from the stone,
Paolo and me, split a sweating Fresca

And walk the eyeless avenues alone.

Grace Lutheran

Spy Wednesday clandestine, Maundy Thursday
Spread a map of the world, a real feast
And such a pleasure after the Lenten fast
That leaves one so hungry and so thirsty.

Downshift the beige Camaro and just drive
Whither the heart will. The heart will wander,
Throbbing with its secret and its wonder.
The world: a hell of a place to be alive!

That he might remove out of this world,
Remove your shoe, I offer you clean feet.
None of the twelve St. Catherines got fat,
Not the one who on the wheel whirled

Until her prayers were answered, and it broke
But the king dispatched her anyway
So she left young and skinny. Anyway,
The axle rose sweetly from the spoke

Of the radio, just as the weather
Turned behind her and opened like a kilt.
The map was shredded and the mood was killed
And upriver the loafing bass wither.

Fowl

The girl from Scarborough liked being slapped
Down the hall from where her mother slept.

A big, hard-working hand, anybody's
To come medicinally down, antibody

To the slow infection of her Western face
(what sucked the most was that it wasn't fast).

Some birds don't migrate. Above, two lonely fowl
Scream across the sky their only vowel.

This river I step in is not the river
I stand in. We'll drive to Leslieville, wherever,

Park in the Guildwood GO lot and get stoned.
Who's there? Nay, answer me. Stand

And unfold yourself. Her heart begins to pound.
No geese go winging to the rooky pond

No goslings disappear their small and speckled.
If we endure this, it will make us special.

Today's Special!

Well I guess that's all locked up tight
Says Sam who guards the mall at night.

Sam's a puppet! He can't use his eyes.
His body is an excellent disguise.

I'm Muffy the Mouse! I'm condemned to rhyme
Until the Christmas special end of time.

That's Jodi, my human friend.
The world goes on and on and will not end

Hiya there Jodi. Oh hi Sam.
Jodi straightens Jeffrey's magic tam.

Everything's safe here let's go upstairs
Sam says through a moustache Props repairs.

Jodi is so pretty. I hate her.
She carries Jeffrey up the escalator

To the kid's department every night
Where he turns into space and starlight

When I say the magic rhyme. Jeff's a mannequin
Until the mall goes dark. Then he's a man again.

King Kong

Attention all stations. Kong's going West.
He's making for the Empire State Building.
A big man in a bad town, short on rest,
Limbs coiling like elevator cabling,

Holding a woman like a remote control,
A blonde which when waved over Manhattan
As a wand, anything might happen—
Around the moon might moan an air patrol,

Three biplanes with machine guns and a cause:
A psychopath who's big and scary too,
So obviously evil, just because,
Demogorgon, muscled, and hairy too.

Black bees bang down, bing steel, and burrow him.
Night flows into his holes, tomorrow, them.
Confused, setting down his unwilling bride,
Kong, on the wrong side of a killing, died.

Mickey Mouse Watch

At midnight he points straight up while you dream,
Harrowing a heaven overhead;
Of two minds, east and west, at nine fifteen,
Then none, hung by a nail above your bed.

At six time bends his smaller hour arm
Out of its joint, but seems to do no harm,
Ascending backwards to time's forward charm
As Mickey's face registers no alarm.

Yorick

Bookending our VHS library
In the basement closet, beside ski suits,
Is our family's one-man Capuchin Crypt,
A skull Dad kept from med school that just sits,
Waiting to be played with, bored, unburied.

Whose skull? A whoreson mad fellow's it was,
The King's jester, whose voice was once so clear,
Clearly a fool for him to end up here.
Maybe someone magnificent, then poor,
Who, if praying, never had a prayer.

I'll hold the skull and think about his life.
Parents who loved him, children, and a wife,
The wind in his face on a summer drive,
His spirit storming through the skull's brief night.
Here is the proof that he was once alive:

His tooth-jeweled jaw, lashed to his skull with springs,
Which I marionette to make him sing
967-1111
Call Pizza Pizza hey hey hey. Heaven
Is here, with me, our suburban basement,

Where, after life's indignities and glory,
Your organs mustered, bequeathed to science,
Having spoken your last words to family
—*Noli Timere, Memento mori*—
You're interred with *The NeverEnding Story.*

Lent

A raccoon rakes
Acorns around
A zoo cage, as a zephyr
Shivers the rocks,
Scatters pine lashes
And ruffles her fur.
A miniature heifer,
A spendthrift, a drifter,
Who spent her summer heft
On winter's warp and weft
Which left her
An angular rack
Draped over with laughter.
She lacked, she waddled
Through Autumn, and after
Clawed down to a burrow
From whence
No call goes.
Then it snowed.
Unconfided,
No one knows
What she sorrowed
— she borrowed, she bided—
Only that she tomorrowed
And tomorrowed and tomorrowed

Gold Nissan

Humans are the only animals
That wipe their asses, or need to. What's done
Is done, the be-all and end-all; the dunnest
Smoke of hell, pocked through like Emmental,
Bubbles upon the table. A ghost may come,
When Mr. Guildwood comes to Dunsinane
To do what's done, and will be done again.

Sleek o'er your rugged looks, my pretty wife,
Be bright and jovial among our guests tonight,
For it is a ghost's right—the beautiful calm—
To likewise haunt the guiltless when he comes.
The hitman and the hangman pay their taxes.
The sun starts shining. Then we parataxis.
The license plate said "Fresh" and there were dice

In the mirror, held up by the last King,
A line that stretches from the crack of doom
Back to the pink bungalow's living room.
And I have a marvelous thing to say,
A certain marvelous thing no one's asking.
For the ingredients in our cauldron,
Severed body parts all—Where are they? Gone?

Super Mario Bros. 3

A mounted cop canters his deputy,
A stallion, through the park. There's too much beauty,

Especially in this world, even now
On a day so Christ-begloomed, in even how

A horse is having fun. You can tell
Music thunders through his muscles just to cancel

A sickle of young grass beneath his hoof.
How else would he love what isn't himself?

Walking at night down Beatrice,
I get a note from the abducted princess.

It's about ghosts. *If you see any ghosts,*
Be careful. The castle where her hosts

Detain her is haunted. The stars are bare
And won't drop super leaves into the air

That could transubstantiate Italians
Into flying raccoons, if not stallions.

The princess warns that ghosts only attack
When you run away from them and don't look back.

Judgement Day

Earth abides. And the sun also rises.
But nothing could prepare me for the shock,
Vanity of vanities, the crisis

Of Arnold beamed down nude between two trucks,
He who had prophesied his endless cycle,
And now was back, and up to his old tricks.

He needs your clothes, your boots, your motorcycle,
But instead gets a cigar to the heart,
Which goes and goes, cold as an icicle.

Dad and I sit in air-conditioned dark,
The popcorn melting like communion,
And the cinema sits in a car park

On a Florida night hot as a kiln.
A molten abstraction becomes a man,
T-1000, who looks like anyone,

Even a Midwestern police officer,
Or your foster mom with a sword for an arm
Who skewers your dad for drinking from the carton.

The devil's in everything. Laid as linoleum,
All he has to do is touch her skin
And then he's her. But something of her charm

Is lost in his cold impersonation.
You catch him by the tingle up your spine—
Her smile inorganic, reptilian,

Too saccharine when she says *Woolfie's fine,*
Woolfie's just fine, dear. John, honey, it's late.
Please don't make me worry. Slamming the pay phone,

Schwarzenegger says: Your foster parents are dead.
Your saviour too is cold, born with a gun,
And will deglove his arm to prove a point:

Not only is evil steel. So is good,
A solid machine forged in fire and quenched,
Austempered to be your personal god,

A real badass, pure Old Testament,
Who'll kill a man for looking at you weird.
I stare up at my dad, whose temperament

Could quicksilver, and hold our tenuous world
On his mercurial surface. Even I,
Annealed with his blood, beaded and bobbed

Across his mirrored pool. Reflecting light
From the screen, T-1000's changes ring,
Weltering upon Dad's human face.

The wind changes direction, rivers run
From the sea, and they've travelled time for you,
The troubled child who might save everyone

With his own cold resolve, on Judgment Day,
August 29th 1997,
When the nascent machinery awakes,

And nukes humanity off to heaven,
Their bodies blown like leaves in the swelter,
Sheltered in a boy's Ferris-black pupil.

Armageddon roars in a smelter—
Schwarzenegger pours liquid nitrogen
Onto the shape shifter, who falters

Then freezes. But a fire in the projection
Booth erupts, as from a SkyNet warhead,
And the film flares and melts at ignition—

Judgment Day. The visible scorched to tephra,
Fusing pyroclastic lapilli white,
The disembodied soundtrack playing on.

The night is igneous. It isn't right.
And in the car, I'm not sure why, I cried.
Dad jokes WE'LL BE BACK, shifts into drive,

And rolls the windows down and then we ride
Down US-41, to the tin sea, where
The sun also sets. And the stars abide.

II

Saturday

Purgatory

In Niagara Falls, Ontario
Marineland is the place to go.
An enchanted land
With a magic man,
Everyone loves Marineland.

You can take your family for the day,
Watching the whales and dolphins play.
Seeing friends you miss,
A great big kiss,
Everyone loves Marineland.

Everyone loves a shining day
And watching the whales while they swim and play.
They jump in the air,
Splashing waves in your hair.
Everyone loves Marineland.

Niagara Falls, Ontario
Is always a fun place to go.
Seeing friends you miss,
A great big kiss,
Everyone loves Marineland.

Maid of the Mist

Lelawala had hardly gone over
And the white man hadn't come with space and time,
When we splashed down in Niagara Falls,
The one from Superman II, where Clark Kent
Goes off for hot dogs and orange juice
As the kid is playing at the railing,
One hand on the wet bar, then the other,
Yelling "Look mom, look mom," before slipping
Soundless into the long unbreaking scream,
Inartfully blending into the green screen.

It had hardly sunk in that we were here,
On a TravelZoo off-season discount,
Flowing up and down Clifton Hill
Where everything looks just like what it is—
A Burger King that looks like Burger King
But with a Frankenstein sign prolapsing
Into a ghost town abandoned by April
But filled with real people eating lunch.
Even the upside-down house museum
Is upside-down both inside and out.

Ask Zoltar in Ripley's Believe It or Not!
He knows everyone, especially strangers,
Happy tourists who feed the prophet loonies,
Parked as he is between two shrunken heads,
Appropriately, for the star of *Big*.
And he cuts you down to size, his turban
The very woop and wharf of space and time,
Enwrapping a great nothing, which knows all,
Especially how to heal old wounds,
And say the things you shouldn't keep inside—

Like Superman, played by Christopher Reeve,
Imprisoned in his own Phantom Zone,
The wax museum, so far from the rail
That in some world the boy keeps falling
Into an inexpertly rendered waterfall,
Schrödinger's cat that neither dies,
Nor lives, nor falls from a black horse
In competitive dressage, and breaks his neck,
And breaks his heart, and breaks his wavy hair,
And breaks this saving, artificial wall.

There goes Lelawala. As we leave,
We try our luck going behind the falls,
The catacombs that snake beneath the gorge.
It costs eleven dollars. There's no line.
And there on the wet concrete wall
Is where the world once ended, with a splash,
When little Roger Woodward, only seven,
Floated downstream without a Superman
Towards his roaring placard on the wall,
Then took a breath, then slipped over the falls,

And when they rescued him he asked for water.

Superman

As a boy, even he played Superman,
Cooking corn until it popped off the cob

By staring at it swaying on its stalk.
Hands on his hips, a red sheet on his back,

Its "S" snapping in the rain-bearing breeze,
His bare feet hovering above Kansas,

He raised himself above the human voices.
His mom, who dressed him as Clark Kent for school,

"So you can get the jump on the bad guys,
And hide in plain sight in this smart disguise,"

Ran out to fetch him like a lost balloon.
"Clark Kent! Come down from there! We're eating soon."

He caught her cancer spun into her lung
Like a spider web, looking down through her.

Once, she'd died. There'd be other women though—
Earthlings all, bound by their soles to earth,

Who had the habit of turning to dirt,
Delicate eggs he'd snatch from their despair

And juggle hand to steel hand through the air
Until they broke, the punchlines of a joke,

His unapplauding hands covered in yolk.
Humanity ripened like mammaries

Among his bumper crop of memories.
Here's one, soft as a peach: laying Lois

Onto the down comforter of her bed,
The bed she was a girl in, her parents

Washing the dishes downstairs and laughing.
Where did she go? Everybody's somewhere,

And anyways that was eons ago,
When human cities still shone below him,

Lite-Brites aspiring to galaxies,
Where real human being used to know him.

He'd condescend to save a special few,
Mostly friends, and friends of friends he knew,

His interventions administrative,
And increasingly to no great effect,

As the whole of them faded into black
Some billion-something years ago today.

He's stopped keeping track. Seasons pass as seconds.
This continent goes green, that one goes white—

He re-imagines Lois's and his fights,
And every million years or so he's right.

He's Superman! He hovers high above.
Once, he remembers something: he was loved.

Or if not loved, then at least diligent,
Thorough, having seen a whole thing through,

His powers fading as the sun goes out,
And he takes his place among the nothing new.

Parkdale, then Princess Street

Make them say yes before you even ask,
L'essence de charme, c'est ça. The mind's a damsel
Locked in a tower with her fathom of hair.
Coax the braid and it'll all be over.

The rooms are plain where I am interviewed,
Abstract and clinical, and so I glory
Like a corpse plant, perfume the marble-faced
With the reek and prodigy of my tomorrows.

Dying is so boring as the soul
Rummages the liquidation sale
For a final bargain.

But time outbids all comers, and we die
Expensively in Princess Margaret
Who was herself once so beautiful.

How droll the selfsame vehicle that drives
Boredom through a day's interstices,
The stopgaps between pigeonholes and doves,

Should waylay—more: should shanghai—both of us
And curb our shouldered duties with a chase.
By your command we freeze in a Boethus,

Boy and goose, locked in a stone détente
Of civic role play blent with violence.
Too soon. Nothing to see here. Moved along

The loved and lonely avenues, violins
Our traffic frets, whose melodies aren't long
For this or any other world, unless

The myths are right, and drag us sight-unseen
Into some upper dream, the officers
Of an all-invigilating task force,

Neatly wrapped, and tied with a green ribbon.
Which, officer, is plainly false. The offenders
Are out there to be sure, deftly riven

Simulacra, sequelled, wreathed in a myst
No headlight can penetrate, on or off.
Therefore we're free to go. Easter's lease

Has far too brief a purchase. Honour, if
It is a thing worth having, has itself,
The way a wolf has moonlight in a whiff.

The Perfect Victim

You tell the poem: do what I fucking say
Or I'm really going to have to hurt you,
Like how Cito's Blue Jays spanked the Yankees
7-6 at the SkyDome this afternoon.

It won't listen. It breaks down and cries,
Dries up, does its best Catholic shy girl bit,
And you're left holding your Bic, unsurprised
That the muse declined your romantic bait.

It won't love you. It won't say, "I love you."
So draw the blinds, unplug the telephone,
Howl away the Easter sun above you,
And see if it really likes being alone.

Every poem wants to be excused.
You follow it into the bathroom
Where your advances are always refused.
Kill your darlings, discard what's bothersome—

The old masters knew it: just crack the thing
With a few hard stanzas, and it'll break
Like a compliant egg, spilling its everything.
What the poem refuses the poet takes.

French Vanilla Ice

To look, to like, to lack, to lock away
Awake, aware, a wreck, and want to walk

Along a lip, a leg, a lap, a ledge
To what, to wit, to wet, to wither where

Alack, a lake, a lock, unless alas
To last, to less, to tease to least, too late

A life, a whelp, aloof, a waif, a wife
At long, at length, alone, at least at last

To lose. Dalheslie. Hell. Hello. Farewell.

Florida

Even the cartoons have come to die
In the swampy penis of the USA
Where clouds resemble naked little girls
Waiting at a bus stop in the sky.
Their kiddy bits are covered by cloud-curls
Which blow, and weren't in the travel guide.
¡At least Latinos actually call you *ese!*

Antony and Cleopatra walk the beach
Like two super good-looking astronauts
In Ken and Barbie spacesuits on a moon
Where Mike Myers is worshiped as a God.
Cleopatra's hot but *such* a bitch
And Ken is Ken in spacesuits on a moon
Straight down, a Matryoshka cosmonaut.

This is a poem about Florida
Before Tamar Dillard was Flo Rida.
Poetry's so old it could retire
Or sink into the Everglade's black cum
And be forgotten like an alligator
When you're skiing an elevator
Shaft double black on Whistler-Blackcomb.

Palm trees have that look, like they would ask
Their victim what she thought about their raps.
Palm trees shouldn't rap. They're not even black!
In town they take machetes to their nuts
And when they peel them open tourists gasp
At the inner guilty nut in its misprision;
On pleasant days it makes you miss prison.

Proserpina

Lucy, Lucy
Little sixpence in a two-piece,
With a Middlesex accent made out of honey
And a head of blonde hair
You can turn into money.

It goes green, it goes green
In the expensive chlorine
Of the Florida pool where I met you.
I'm Marco. You're Polo.
And I dare you, I bet you

Don't care, you don't care
That your parents aren't fair
And your sister's in high school
And everyone likes you,
Your GameBoy, your cool.

To your condo, your condo
While your dad is out golfing,
To eat pomegranates you arm like grenades,
And sit on your sofa,
Watch *Doug* and then *Rugrats*.

But you're sleepy, you're sleepy
And you promise you'll write me
As an afternoon storm with its thunder and lightning
Shuts off the TV
Which was telling us something.

4.16

The King had tired of our national perfection of euphemism. He foresaw big things in lying, and in love, and had a hunch that his ladies could do better than this politesse gussied up with Yorkville and luxury. He got off on the truth, that dead hour of desire and Swiss Chalet. Even if it was an abnegation of piety, he burned for it. He commanded, if nothing else, an essentially human power.

Lots of women who knew him had been murdered. Pour Chalet Sauce onto the garden of beauty! Beneath the sword, something happened. They went. He ordered no replacements—The women recurred.

He killed his subjects, after recording his rhymes or after drinking—the retards all followed his directions.

He had a hobby: putting down thoroughbreds. Extreme close-up! He burned Grace Lutheran to the ground. He pounced on strangers, and hacked their bodies up. —The unsuspecting crowds, the Bass loafers, the beautiful animals all endured.

Can Smiley Faces Smile Amid Ruin, or: can we be restored by sadism? Nobody said a word. No one dared the consolation of a thought.

One night he drove out, thinking. A Genie appeared; she could smile and wiggle her nose. She radiated the promise of a various and complex love! of a nameless, even unspeakable love! Then the King and the Genie vanished, probably into the general health. The Have-A-Nap, or wherever—who actually gives a shit? Therefore—ergo—they died together.

Actually, no (spoiler alert!): the King would later die in the fortress he'd achieve, at a natural age, in the City of Kings, not even torn to pieces and his severed head still rapping. The King was the Genie. The Genie was the King.

Glen Gould has abandoned our honestly who the fuck cares

The Have-A-Nap Motel

from the Occitan

A bloated lady
Lay bloating in a road;
A bloated belly
She bore;
Bloated hands
And bloated feet,
Bloated meat
That ready;
Bloated bat
And bloated blade
That ready.
Follow the pain
From bone to sinew
[*missing*   ]
From skin to hair
From hair to meadow,
Where the Scarborough assumes it
And continues

Radar

The bear was named after the guy from M*A*S*H,
The incorrigible troll with ESP,
Hearing as fine as a woman's eyelash

And a revolving roster of spy holes
That opened onto the nurses' shower
Precipitating above an eyeball.

His voice went out from the PA tower,
And once, emboldened by Hawkeye's beer,
He read the day's announcements out in Morse.

That's Radar. I named him. He is my bear,
A foot tall, eyes black and patient as pearls
On a head that revolves like Linda Blair's

In *The Exorcist.* Today wet snow whirls
The windshield, close to collapsing to rain,
As we drive into upper-middle Oakville,

Unfinished neighbourhoods supervised by cranes,
Sapling-lined streets that segue into farms,
Whole subdivisions sprouting up like grains.

Our Mazda slowing, Radar in my arms,
We pull up to a half-constructed house,
Where, in the driveway, sits my cousins' car.

Auntie Lori and Uncle Bob get out,
Then Ryan and Jenn. This is their new house,
A Tyvek ghost, the front door's mouth a shout

Muffled by wafting plastic to a hiss.
I'm nine years old, the same age as Dante
When he trembled, first seeing Beatrice,

But here am I, playing with a Teddy.
Embarrassed, I leave Radar on the porch,
And walk into the house, which isn't ready,

The second floor not staircased to the first,
The winds of Easter blowing hard through it,
A Lethe quenching the plywood ground's thirst,

The only element alien to it
Being the human. I turn left to leave,
Open my mouth to scream but can't do it,

My voice barred by what my eyes can't believe:
Radar is gone, Radar, my best friend,
Whose very body was my own relief,

On whom I turned my back for a second.
How could he not have seen his captor coming,
He whose namesake could detect the sucking

Thumps of a chopper as distant humming?
Or did he see it through his locked-in syndrome,
The very spirit of Oakville homing

His unattended signal, a scapegoat
For the sins of his namesake, his black eyes
Unblinking at the oncoming caped ghost?

We search for him an hour, but surprise:
He's gone. Driving home, dad says he likes Oakville
As the snow turns into rain. Then mom cries

As CBC reports a missing girl,
And I understand where Radar's gone. Of course:
To go retrieve her for us, our new world,

As the National Research Council, in Morse,
Indicates it's exactly one o'clock:
Short short short, long long long, short short short.

III

Sunday

The Devil

Something is happening.
The smell of shit, or meat
Rotting. Hell at least cooled

And forestalled ripening.
Heaven is warm and sweet
As a corpse freshly killed.

Something is opening.
The earth's winter orbit
Aborted, life is called

From its hibernating.
Come, Lazarus, and eat.
Your breakfast will get cold.

Claw at your fastenings,
And crawl, Christ, up Grace Street
With your hair Karly curled,

Stinking and singing. Spring—
Cast out like a goat
I cried and cried.

Capri

Lunch is wholly irresponsible,
The sun hovering worse than any waiter,
Scrutinizing every guilty course,
As Mount Vesuvius attends the water
Like a bulimic who prepares, on principle,
To pumice the Bay of Naples with its curse.

Today's seccondi special, their claws bound,
Is lobster flown straight in from Canada
Which blushes when you put it on the spot.
Grow a backbone! The lid entombs them, live,
Like the sealed lips of a girl's barrette
That shuts its mouth on what she can forget.

She can sit and enjoy lunch without regret,
Or even nausea, imagining Naples
Struggling like an oiled egret
Below Vesuvius's hemorrhaging nipples.
She orders *frutti di bosca* gelato
And reserves a tour of the Blue Grotto.

The sea rides up. The grotto disappears.
Then falls the boat-jeweled gymslip, and it clears—
The entrance to some birth canal, or grave.
Kanye says: May all your pain be Champaign,
All your lunches sponsored by Champlain.
The boatman draws his oars and grabs the chain

Then pulls some screaming girls into the cave.

The Scarborough Grace

An old man on Grace Street is going mad
In a *Canadian* t-shirt he won't change
And red unwrinkling pants I thought had made
Him stylish when I met him in the spring—

Five or six times a day I see him walk
Down Grace Street to St. Francis church, and knock
And pull its wooden doors, always shocked
That his entitled holy place is locked.

Undreams Damascus from a baffled Paul
Rolls back the road where some unstricken Saul
Rises up, as bubbles through a beer
To a surface where we disappear

And wake in some uncalendared forever,
An unwelcome Elijah passing over

Holy Cross

She is prepared to dissociate mind
From body, the worst marriage in the universe,
Worse even than pairing red wine with mint,

Which goes with nothing, the husbandry perverse.
The Devil, on Easter Sunday, insane,
Approaches Christ in Hell with two perfumes:

It's time, he says, to play the Perfume Game.
Christ is dead at this point, so she stinks,
But her mind is so vacant that her name

Is being pampered somewhere in the sticks,
Sponge-bathed of its worries, warm, and wrapped
In terrycloth, staring at sunflower stalks.

Pick the right one and you won't get rapped
About the ears by me, the Devil says
In the rhythmic way that suggests he raps.

Satan's helpers, Mint and Beaujolais,
Each take a bottle and show it to Christian.
One bottle reads Escape, one Eternity.

The mirror splits Satan into Tristan
And Iseult, each more beautiful than insult
Added to injury, combined, and tanned,

Well rested after the weekend's assault.
Eternity, Christ says, and reaches out
To what and where and who and when and how?

This is the earth and I am on it now.

Easter Parade

What is there to know about dying?
It parks over whatever you're doing,
A nimbus that brings rain up from the Earth
And gathers us back in a storm of voices
That thunders on about our mortal vices.

The wind sounds like goats that sound like people,
Not like ghosts, which neither howl nor hover.
Two things equal to the same thing are equal,
As wind and people are, to each other.
Then comes the marching band up Beatrice

Who even as a girl was walked all over
By sandaled local men in costume
And bystanding widows who'll wear forever
The black that survives grief but not custom.
Behind the band, the same man has played Christ

For twenty years. He worries that he's aged.
He wants a face as empty as a page,
Unwritten by the lines of getting old.
Who wants to see an old Christ in the cold
Being whipped by Romans on College Street,

Pain faked uncannily with real wrinkles?
This will be the year he doesn't flinch
As they mush him down Grace Street in shackles
Past the school for children who speak French.
His face, which braves each lash for vanity,

The stoic image of Christ's sanity.

Lot's Wife

Overcome—but the zombies started slowly,
First one and then another, like houseguests
Just boozily strolling across the park
Where the softball beer leagues were still at play
At seven forty-five on a Sunday.

Overcome by the ordinary sight
Of two figures just walking up Bellwoods,
Into the middle of our life's twilight,
Hesitating at Henderson, and then
Bearing down on Grace Street again,

I called you from your cooking to the porch,
The best porch in Toronto, which you love,
And yelled to pack, and that we had to leave.
God is coming down from off his perch
And the zombies were already past the church

When the cabbie showed up, and honked us down,
With strict instructions not to turn around
As the dead patted the trunk like wet leaves.
Then beside me came the exquisite sound
Of a hillock of salt dumped on the ground—

You turned, and saw the zombies' faces: ours.
Having been alone now for many years,
Days in the sandglass rotate mirror to mirror.
Every savory thing I taste is yours;
I turn the salt mill and shake out my hours.

Heaven

The house where it happened has been erased,
The lot at Bayview and Christie renumbered.
Christie, which at home turns into Grace,
Here just blanks where the lake remembers.

I've come on the day of an open house
Two lots from where it happened, on Christie.
Christie, which at home turns into Grace,
Here will only ever be Christie.

I park the car and walk Port Dalhousie,
A place I've thought a lot about lately,
Up Christie, which at home turns into Grace,
As surely as spring segues snow to grass.

Port Dalhousie is a beautiful place!
A lot prettier than I remember.
Even Christie, which at home turns into Grace,
But here divides without a remainder.

You can see Toronto across the lake
From a little parkette with two benches
Past Christie, which at home turns into Grace,
Where today a couple sits and frenches.

The perfect island cottages efface
The reason why I've come to St. Catherine's:
To visit Christie, which at home feeds Grace,
But here is appointed with quaint cabins.

I turn and walk toward where the house was razed,
Discreetly taking a few photographs,
Toward Christie, which at home turns into Grace,
But find myself feeling the scaredy cat,

Fearing that each window secrets a face
Staring out on a stranger with designs
On Christie, which at home turns into Grace,
When a voice surprises me from behind:

"Something photogenic about this place?"
It is a woman, white-haired and wizened,
Five houses from Christie, reclining back
On the roof of her bed and breakfast.

I suddenly recall the women of Thrace
Who knew that Orpheus can't be forgiven,
Not for looking at hell, but at her face,
So as he sang, they ripped him to ribbons.

I stutter and offer a weird grimace.
The disabusing lie can't help me here.
Here, art itself is inappropriate,
As am I, with my rattle bag of puns.

Plus I have a secret telling would debase,
One I hope will transform insanity
Into Christie, the corridor of Grace,
Condescend into our inanity

And redeem the nightmare of innocence—
To pave the death-swept swampland, in a sense,
Into Christie, which somehow becomes Grace,
Where streetlamps hum you home behind their glass.

And so I lie, with my guilt-screwed-up face:
"No, I was just here for the open house,
On Christie. The house looks pretty damn great!
I'm just photographing the neighbourhood."

"What open house?" She asks. I'm a disgrace.
Had I imagined it? I start to sweat.
"The one on Christie." Time turns into space
As she stares down at me incredulous

And I panic, and make toward the hell place,
Sandwiching myself between the lie
And Christie, which at home becomes Grace.
And all I want to do is run away,

Run back through the years the years erase,
Run from this street which still terrifies
With Christie, and with my hope for her Grace,
Run screaming back before even Christ dies

And disfigures death with the hope of Grace.
Grace, which is the very thing death takes
Into the perfect house art can't deface
With the perfecting hope that death awakes.

At the End of the Day

from Baudelaire's French

In the wan and waning twilight
Life goes on spitefully, goes on
Its endless riot, no mind to right.
The sun abandons the horizon

And night voluptuously rises,
Packing in its velvet valise
Our baggage, shame, and all malaise.
I'm one of its surprises—

Still sick in love with mankind
And ready for bed. Here I go,
With first drafts of dreams in my mind

And a queen-sized fit for a king,
Bedding begging for a wallow,
Where I'll toss and turn into nothing.

Ghost

You're gone by dinner, then I'm tucked in bed,
And I can hear the spring's first birds outside,

Home from the innumerable nations
And fearsome governments of migration.

Our oak is filling up with chickadees,
Plying the air with their two-tone trochees,

And the whole night, warm with medical spring,
Bends in to hear the haunted oak tree sing:

You'll never end up growing old, or grey,
Or living long enough to be cliché.

Time warps too. I'm back in my pajamas,
And dad reads "The Ghost and Jenny Jemima."

The clock struck one, the clock struck two,
The ghost came playing peekaboo,

And the chickadees and the ghost sing too
Wa-OOO wa-OOO wa-OOO wa-OOO wa-OOO.

Equally around me lays my whole life,
And somewhere ages and miles on, my wife,

A stranger tucked in her childhood bed,
Or like Jemima running from the spread

Of a white human blob climbing her stairs—
Jemima, who peeking through her fingers,

Looks like the beautiful girl from the news
And even now is travelling to you.

Tenebrae

for KF

Words escaped me when it was time to wish.
Dumbfounded before my birthday candles
The day he was convicted in his shackles,
And I stopped dressing up as Superman,
I knew there was a word, but just not which,

Grasping gripless like grass at grass—gone,
Gobsmacked in the cordilleric light
Of twelve candles balletic in a night
Made more damasked by the wind's augury.
The feeling blazes in its filament,

Lights blue the pool where we were fingering
Blindly for each other at Marco Polo,
Fades as sleep eddying under your pillow,
But its name vanishes without a trace.
I huff and puff, and blow the flickering

Flames to smoke scintillas. But one flame stays:
Light of the world. My wish. My missing word,
Which couldn't have been spoken, only heard—
The inextinguishable ache of this place,
Earth, in whose light I turn and see your face.

ACKNOWLEDGEMENTS

I'm grateful to the editors of the magazines and anthologies where these poems first appeared:

The Walrus and *The Best Canadian Poetry 2012:* "The Scarborough Bluffs"

Poetry: "Fowl," "Today's Special," "Parkdale, Then Princess Street," and "The Scarborough Grace"

Taddle Creek: "The Perfect Victim"

Hazlitt: "Radar"

Thanks to The Ontario Arts Council, for Writers Reserve and Work-in-Progress grants, and for nominating these poems for a K.M. Hunter Award. To my family: Mum, Dad, and Beb. To Josh. And to Jason Guriel and Carmine Starnino.

Carmine Starnino, Editor
Michael Harris, Founding Editor